D0894351

American Symbols
AND THEIR Meanings

THE CONFEDERATE FLAG

American Symbols AND THEIR Meanings

THE
CONFEDERATE
FLAG

HAL MARCOVITZ

MASON CREST PUBLISHERS
PHILADELPHIA

First printing

1 3 5 7 9 8 6 4 2

Library of Congress Cataloging-in-Publication Data
on file at the Library of Congress

ISBN 1-59084-035-6

Publisher's note: all quotations in this book come
from original sources, and contain the spelling and
grammatical inconsistencies of the original text.

American Symbols
AND THEIR Meanings

CONTENTS

Introduction

THE IMPORTANCE OF AMERICAN SYMBOLS

Symbols are not merely ornaments to admire—they also tell us stories. If you look at one of them closely, you may want to find out why it was made and what it truly means. If you ask people who live in the society in which the symbol exists, you will learn some things. But by studying the people who created that symbol and the reasons why they made it, you will understand the deepest meanings of that symbol.

The United States owes its identity to great events in history, and the most remarkable American Symbols are rooted in these events. The struggle for independence from Great Britain gave America the Declaration of Independence, the Liberty Bell, the American flag, and other images of freedom. The War of 1812 gave the young country a song dedicated to the flag, "The Star-Spangled Banner," which became our national anthem. Nature gave the country its national animal, the bald eagle. These symbols established the identity of the new nation, and set it apart from the nations of the Old World.

To be emotionally moving, a symbol must strike people with a sense of power and unity. But it often takes a long time for a new symbol to be accepted by all the people, especially if there are older symbols that have gradually lost popularity. For example, the image of Uncle Sam has replaced Brother Jonathan, an earlier representation of the national will, while the Statue of Liberty has replaced Columbia, a woman who represented liberty to Americans in the early 19th century. Since then, Uncle Sam and the Statue of Liberty have endured and have become cherished icons of America.

Of all the symbols, the Statue of Liberty has perhaps the most curious story, for unlike other symbols, Americans did not create her. She was created by the French, who then gave her to America. Hence, she represented not what Americans thought of their country but rather what the French thought of America. It was many years before Americans decided to accept this French goddess of Liberty as a symbol for the United States and its special role among the nations: to spread freedom and enlighten the world.

This series of books is valuable because it presents the story of each of America's great symbols in a freshly written way and will contribute to the students' knowledge and awareness of them. It is to be hoped that this information will awaken an abiding interest in American history, as well as in the meanings of American symbols.

—*Barry Moreno,*
librarian and historian
Ellis Island/Statue of Liberty National Monument

The crew of the Confederate steamship *Shenandoah* were the last Confederates to surrender at the end of the Civil War. General Robert E. Lee surrendered his army while the ship was at sea, and the sailors on the *Shenandoah* did not receive the news until they were told by a passing British ship.

VOYAGE OF THE *SHENANDOAH*

The *Sea King* was a fast steamship that arrived in the Madeira Islands off the coast of Africa in October 1864. It had left London 10 days before. Along the way the ship met up with a supply ship carrying guns and ammunition. Also on board was Captain James Waddell, an officer in the navy of the Confederate States of America.

In port in Madeira, Waddell's job was to turn the *Sea King* into a fighting *vessel* in the Confederate Navy. He would then take over as the ship's commander. Waddell supervised the placement of guns and ammunition aboard the *Sea King* and made the ship ready for combat.

He also renamed the *Sea King*. It became known as the Confederate States Ship (C.S.S.) *Shenandoah*.

When the ship and crew were ready, Waddell guided the *Shenandoah* west out of Madeira, across the Atlantic Ocean toward the coast of New England. Its mission was to sink whaling ships that were heading home with their rich cargoes of whale fat, called blubber.

High atop one of the *Shenandoah*'s masts flew the ship's colors—its battle flag. Known as the Confederate Navy Jack, it included the Southern Cross flag. This consisted of a blue cross containing 13 stars set against a red field. The Southern Cross flag had been carried into battle by Confederate soldiers since early in the war. In the navy flag, the Southern Cross flag was set on a white background.

The hunting was good for the *Shenandoah*. Waddell's ship sank six Union vessels in a little more than three weeks of sailing. On November 12, 1864, the *Shenandoah* turned south and headed toward South America. Along the way, Waddell's ship encountered three more Union vessels and sank them all. By the end of 1864, the *Shenandoah* had sailed around Cape Horn on the tip of South America and headed north. Its captain intended to sink Union whaling ships bound for Hawaii.

Although the *Shenandoah* was having great success at sea, early in 1865 the Confederate Army suffered a series of defeats. It now appeared the war would soon be over. On April 9, 1865, General Robert E. Lee, the commander of the Confederate Army, surrendered to Union General Ulysses S. Grant at Appomattox Court House in Virginia. This marked the end of the Civil War, although some Confederates continued to fight.

While the *Shenandoah* was out to sea, its captain had no idea the war was drawing to a close. Through March and April 1865 the *Shenandoah* continued its attacks on whaling ships in the Pacific Ocean, wreaking havoc on merchant shipping. Even after the end of the war, the *Shenandoah* continued to sink whaling ships. On June 22, while sailing north of Japan in the Bering Sea, the *Shenandoah* encountered the whaler *Jerah Swift*, which was based in New Bedford, Massachusetts. The *Shenandoah* fired one of its big cannons at the *Jerah Swift* and scored a direct hit. Waddell had no idea that he had just fired the final shot in the Civil War.

Several weeks later, a merchant ship showed Captain Waddell a newspaper story about the surrender of the **Confederacy**. When he read the news, Waddell sailed for England in an effort to avoid capture by the U. S. Navy. On November 6, 1865—seven months after the surrender of General Lee—the *Shenandoah* arrived in port in Liverpool, England, still flying the Confederate flag.

The flag was lowered. It would never again fly as the official flag of a nation on Earth.

"I claim for her officers and men a triumph over their enemies and over every obstacle," Captain Waddell wrote. "For myself, I claim having done my duty."

CHARLESTON

MERCURY

EXTRA:

Passed unanimously at 1.15 o'clock, P. M., December
20th, 1860.

AN ORDINANCE

To dissolve the Union between the State of South Carolina and
other States united with her under the compact entitled "The
Constitution of the United States of America."

We, the People of the State of South Carolina, in Convention assembled, do declare and ordain, and
it is hereby declared and ordained,

That the Ordinance adopted by us in Convention, on the twenty-third day of May, in the
year of our Lord one thousand seven hundred and eighty-eight, whereby the Constitution of the
United States of America was ratified, and also, all Acts and parts of Acts of the General
Assembly of this State, ratifying amendments of the said Constitution, are hereby repealed;
and that the union now subsisting between South Carolina and other States, under the name of
"The United States of America," is hereby dissolved.

THE

UNION

IS

DISSOLVED!

The front page of the Charleston *Mercury* newspaper on December 20, 1860, shouts the news that South Carolina intended to leave the United States. In the next few weeks, six other Southern states also voted to leave the Union. These states decided to band together and form their own nation, the Confederate States of America.

THE STARS AND BARS

he notion that the Confederacy would need its own flag was raised in Montgomery, Alabama, in February 1861, as **delegates** from Southern states that had decided to leave the Union gathered to write a charter for their new government.

The Confederate **Congress** met in the Alabama State House. Jefferson Davis had just been elected the first **president** of the Confederacy. He appointed a committee to design a Great Seal, Coat of Arms, motto, and flag. William Porcher Miles, a delegate from South Carolina, was made chairman of what became known as the Flag and Seal Committee.

The committee soon found itself swamped with ideas. The first designs were proposed by Christopher G. Memminger, a delegate from South Carolina. One of Memminger's designs called for a blue cross of seven stars on a red field. Memminger said the design was based on the *constellation* known as the Southern Cross. The stars stood for the seven states that sent delegates to the Confederate Congress—South Carolina, Mississippi, Florida, Alabama, Georgia, Louisiana and Texas.

Memminger submitted similar designs that contained as many as 15 stars to represent the slave-holding states that had not sent delegates to the Confederate Congress—Virginia, Arkansas, Tennessee and North Carolina, as well as Maryland, which attempted to *secede* but was prevented by federal troops to ensure the safety of the federal *capital* in Washington, D.C.; Delaware, a slave state that remained loyal to the Union; and Kentucky and Missouri, which had both Confederate and Union governments. Memminger said it was his hope every slave state would soon join in "the glorious constellation of our Southern Confederacy."

Miles and the other members of the flag committee were not prepared to accept Memminger's designs. Some members of the Confederate Congress saw no reason the Confederacy should not adopt the Stars and Stripes as the flag as well as the "The Star-Spangled Banner" by Francis Scott Key as the national anthem of the South. President Davis and many delegates to the

Confederate Congress believed the South had just as much right as the North to "Old Glory," the Stars and Stripes.

Over the next month the flag committee received proposed designs for the new flag from several delegates. Eventually, Miles and the other committee members found themselves considering some 120 designs for the new flag. The flag committee rejected all the designs submitted by the delegates and decided to look elsewhere. In its report to the Confederate Congress, the committee wrote: "A flag should be simple, readily made, and, above all, capable of being made up in *bunting*; it should

William Porcher Miles, a deputy to the Confederate Congress from South Carolina, was appointed by Confederate President Jefferson Davis to head the Flag and Seal Committee. His committee eventually approved the design for the Stars and Bars. Later, while serving on the staff of General Beauregard, Miles helped design the Southern Cross battle flag.

He was born in 1822 in Waterloo, South Carolina, and graduated from the College of Charleston in South Carolina in 1842. In 1855, he was elected mayor of Charleston. Miles was elected to the U.S. Congress in 1857, where he supported slavery and secession. He left Washington in 1860.

In 1863, Miles married Betty Beirne, daughter of Oliver Beirne, a wealthy owner of plantations in Virginia and Louisiana. Following the war, Miles managed his father-in-law's plantations in Louisiana, overseeing them and living quietly until his death in 1899.

be different from the flag of any other country, place or people; it should be significant; it should be readily distinguishable at a distance; the colors should be well contrasted and durable; and lastly, and not the least important point, it should be effective and handsome."

The flag the committee finally picked was not that much different from the Stars and Stripes.

Mrs. Napoleon Lockett, the daughter of Alabama Governor Andrew B. Moore, knew an artist and teacher named Niccola Marschall who lived in nearby Marion, Alabama. She asked Marschall to propose a design. The artist quickly sketched three designs, one of which showed three wide horizontal stripes of equal width. The two outer stripes were red while the inside stripe was white. In the upper left corner he placed a field of

This sheet music for a song about the Confederate Flag was dedicated to Confederate president Jefferson Davis. Written in early 1861, the cover features the newly designed "Stars and Bars" flag of the Confederacy.

blue with a circle of seven stars. Mrs. Lockett showed it to the committee. There was no question the Marschall design bore considerable similarity to Old Glory. However, the design was quickly adopted as the

> The first ship to fly the Stars and Bars following secession was the *Pearl*, which sailed for Antigua on March 5, 1861. When the ship arrived in port, angry New England sailors tore the Stars and Bars from its mast.

first official flag of the Confederate States of America.

The first Confederate flag was sewn March 2 by a *seamstress* in Montgomery, Alabama. The committee's plan was to unveil the new flag—which became known as the Stars and Bars—on March 4, 1861, the day Abraham Lincoln would take the oath of office as president of the United States in Washington, D.C.

On that day, a huge crowd gathered outside the Alabama State House. President Davis decided to give the honor of raising the first flag of the Confederacy to Letitia C. Tyler, the granddaughter of former U.S. President John Tyler, who had been a delegate to the Confederate Congress.

At just past 4 P.M., a brass band started to play the anthem of the Confederacy, "Dixie." Standing below a flagpole on the *Capitol* grounds, Letitia drew down on the *halyard*, and the Stars and Bars flag was hoisted over the cheering crowd.

Union and Confederate troops clash at the Battle of Franklin, Tennessee, in November 1864. Soon after the Civil War began, the Confederates adopted a new flag to carry into battle, featuring a blue cross with thirteen white stars on a red background. This battle flag, also known as the Southern Cross, has become the most recognizable symbol of the Confederacy.

THE SOUTHERN CROSS

ithin days, the new Stars and Bars flag was flying across the Confederacy. Hastily made copies were stitched together and flown over the capital buildings of the rebellious states. Ships anchored in Confederate harbors flew the flag atop their masts. Newspapers published in the South featured images of the flag on their *mastheads*. In Montgomery, Alabama, the Confederate Congress ordered an enormous version made for the Capitol measuring 28 feet by 18 feet.

Early in the morning of April 12—just five weeks after the flag was hoisted over the Capitol in Montgomery—southern troops fired on a Union force guarding Fort Sumter in the harbor of Charleston, South Carolina. The first shots of the Civil War had been launched. Soon armies wearing Union blue or Confederate gray would clash during four years of bloody, tragic fighting.

The attack on Fort Sumter was led by a Confederate general named Pierre Gustave Toutant Beauregard. The

General Pierre Beauregard was one of the first heroes of the South—he commanded the artillery brigade that bombarded Fort Sumter with cannon shots, thus touching off the Civil War in April 1861. Months later, at the Battle of First Manassas, he was instrumental in routing the Union Army, delivering the South's first important victory.

Beauregard was born in St. Bernard Parish, Louisiana. He was trained as a soldier at the U.S. Military Academy at West Point and fought in the Mexican War during the late 1840s. He resigned from the U.S. Army in 1861 to join the Confederate Army.

Not all his battles during the Civil War were Southern victories. He lost the important Battle of Shiloh, and was relieved of command of the Confederate Army in Tennessee. He was placed in charge of troops defending the coastlines of Georgia and South Carolina. Late in the war Beauregard was again given command of an army, and helped slow the advance of the Union Army toward Richmond, Virginia.

Following the war, Beauregard returned to Louisiana and became president of a railroad. He died in New Orleans in 1893.

soldiers inside the fort withstood bombardment from Beauregard's guns for nearly two days, then surrendered. Beauregard emerged from the short battle as the first hero of the Confederacy.

Two months later, the armies of the North and South clashed near Manassas, Virginia. Unlike Fort Sumter, in which no one injured or killed, Manassas was a bloody battle that featured many *casualties*. Thousands of soldiers on foot and horseback slammed into each other on July 21, 1861.

Generals found themselves in the field directing *strategies* and *tactics*. One of those generals was Beauregard. His troops were pinned down along a road known as the Warrenton Turnpike. In front of Beauregard's troops was a large force of Union soldiers. General Beauregard wanted to attack, but he needed more men to hold his position while his soldiers charged the Union lines. Late in the afternoon, Beauregard received a dispatch from his signal officer, Captain Edward P. Alexander, reporting an approaching force of soldiers in the rear. Unfortunately, they were flying a red, white, and blue flag. Alexander said he could not tell whether it was the Stars and Bars, or if they were Northern troops.

There was little breeze, meaning the banners carried by the troops hung straight and lifeless. What's more, the dust kicked up by the troops, wagons and horses obscured everyone's vision.

This 19th century illustration shows Union troops charging the Confederate lines at Manassas. Note the similarities in the American flag at left and in the Confederate Stars and Bars flag at the right.

Soon, General Beauregard could see the approaching soldiers for himself. Unfortunately, he could not identify whether they were Union or Confederate soldiers, either.

"General Beauregard tried again and again to decide what colors they carried," wrote Carlton McCarthy, a private in the Confederate Army. "He used his glass repeatedly, and handing it to others begged them to look, hoping their eyes might be keener than his."

Beauregard had to make a decision. Should he hold his ground on the chance the troops were on his side? Or should he order a withdrawal? If he remained, and the troops turned out to be Union, his men would surely be caught in a trap between the two large Northern armies.

"Suddenly, a puff of wind spread the colors to the breeze," wrote McCarthy. "It was the Confederate flag—the Stars and Bars. The moment the flag was recognized, Beauregard turned to his staff, right and left, saying, 'See that the day is ours!' and ordered an immediate advance."

The Confederate forces charged into the Union lines. Beauregard's attack helped turn the tide that day in favor of the South, which won what would come to be known as the First Battle of Manassas. It is also called the First Battle of Bull Run. A second battle took place at the same place in August 1862.

Manassas may have been a great victory for the South, but Beauregard knew that it could have been a defeat if he had guessed wrong about the color of the approaching flag. Clearly, he knew, the Southern troops would need a distinctive and colorful banner to carry onto the battlefields against the Union soldiers. He discussed the issue with other Confederate military leaders. They agreed that a different flag was needed.

Beauregard proposed a new battle flag similar to the

> Many Confederate battle flags were sewn from a supply of red material captured from a Union warehouse at a Navy base in Norfolk, Virginia; therefore, the North supplied the material for a lot of the South's flags.

banner suggested by Christopher Memminger some months before. Other generals learned of Beauregard's plans and recommended designs as well. Finally, Beauregard had his *regiment*'s mapmaker draw a flag that depicted a banner with a blue cross, white stars, and a red field.

In their correspondence, Beauregard and the other generals referred to the new flag as "St. Andrew's Cross." St. Andrew, a follower of Jesus Christ, had been put to death by the Romans on a cross nailed together in the shape of an "X." The cross was also known as the saltire, and had been adopted as the flag of Scotland.

On the Confederate battle flag, the blue cross included 13 stars, even though at this point only 11 states had seceded from the Union. On the battle flag, the two extra stars represented Kentucky and Missouri. There was no question that the bold and brilliant red flag could be recognized in the field by soldiers on both sides of the battle, no matter how little wind there was, or how much dust was kicked up by the horses and wagons.

This is the Confederate battle flag, with its "southern cross" and 13 stars. During the Civil War many Confederate battle flags were square rather than rectangular; it was believed the square shape would save silk, which was hard to find in the South.

The War Department approved the change. Confederate soldiers would now go into battle under the Southern Cross. Officers and men of the Confederate army greeted the new flag with enthusiasm.

Meanwhile, the Confederate Congress had grown increasingly dissatisfied with the Stars and Bars. Both delegates and Confederate citizens complained that a flag of red and white stripes and cluster of stars on a blue

---

Christopher G. Memminger, a delegate to the Confederate Congress from South Carolina, had suggested a flag based on the Southern Cross. He was turned down by the flag committee, which instead approved the Stars and Bars. Later, his design found its way onto the Confederate Army's battle flags, and by the end of the Civil War the Southern Cross was the most recognizable symbol of the South.

After the war started, Memminger had little time to involve himself in the debate over the flag. Confederate President Jefferson Davis appointed him secretary of the treasury, meaning it was Memminger's responsibility to collect money to pay for the war.

He was able to raise money from citizens of the South by selling war bonds. The government of the Confederate States of America issued the bonds with the promise to repay the money with interest to the citizens after the war. Of course, the government did not survive the war, so people who bought the bonds had no way to get their money back.

Today, Confederate bonds are likely to be worth a lot of money to collectors, but many people who lived in the South during the war and supported the Confederate government lost their life savings by buying the bonds.

26 The Confederate Flag

Three of the flags used by the Confederacy: The original Stars and Bars is on the top; a later version of this flag had a circle of 12 stars in the blue field, with a larger star in the center. In 1863 the Stars and Bars was replaced by the Stainless Banner, which featured the battle flag on a field of white. In the Confederacy's final flag, a vertical red stripe was added to the Stainless Banner; however, few of these flags were made because the Civil War ended about a month after this new flag was unveiled.

field resembled the American flag—the emblem of a country they had grown to hate.

On May 1, 1863, the Confederate government replaced the Stars and Bars with a second national flag. The new flag was a white banner with the Southern Cross placed in the upper left corner.

This flag was known as the "Stainless Banner." Some troops in the field adopted the new flag and carried it in battle, but when there was no wind and the flag drooped on its pole, it was difficult to see the Southern Cross. When this happened, the Stainless Banner appeared as nothing more than a white flag, which in battle is the flag of surrender.

In early 1865, even though the Civil War was nearly over, the Confederate Congress decided to create a new flag. This flag, adopted on March 8, 1865, was very similar to the Stainless Banner, but it now included a broad vertical red stripe along the outer edge of the banner.

General Thomas J. "Stonewall" Jackson died from a wound he received at the Battle of Chancellorsville; he was buried in Lexington, Kentucky, in a coffin draped with one of the Stainless Banners. After his funeral the Stainless Banner was sometimes referred to as the "Jackson Flag."

By now, though, the Civil War was just weeks away from its conclusion. After four years of war, there was little food, ammunition, or raw materials left in the South. Certainly, whatever fabrics were available were needed to make and mend clothes of the citizens and returning soldiers. Few copies of the final flag were stitched and displayed.

A Confederate soldier's grave is decorated with a battle flag. In the years following the war, citizens of both the North and the South set aside a day at the end of May to decorate the graves of soldiers with flowers and flags. Originally called Decoration Day, it has become the national holiday on which we honor all those who have fought for the United States, Memorial Day.

"DYE IT WITH YOUR BLOOD!"

By the end of 1861, the Southern Cross battle flag was a familiar sight at the head of Confederate armies. Many of those first flags did not feature red fields behind the cross of stars, but a pink or rose-colored background. When Confederate Army officers complained about the color to Beauregard, he barked: "Dye it red sir, dye it with your blood!"

The flag was often dyed with the blood of the flag bearer. It was a great honor to be chosen to carry the flag into battle, but it was also one of the most dangerous jobs in the regiment. The flag bearer was unable to carry a gun, and he found himself an easy target because enemy

According to Confederate legend, the first three Southern Cross battle flags were stitched by sisters Hetty and Jennie Cary of Baltimore, Maryland, and their cousin, Constance Cary, of Alexandria, Virginia. The Cary women are said to have sewn the flags from material they obtained by taking apart their fancy party dresses.

In later years, historians found letters written by Constance Cary, in which she describes the first flags made of red and blue silk, and how difficult it was to obtain the material. That would suggest the flags were not made from the ladies' dresses. They would be quite easy to find hanging in their closets.

In any event, it appears the Cary sisters and their cousin presented the first three flags to Generals Earl Van Dorn, Joseph Johnston, and Pierre Beauregard. When Van Dorn died during a battle in Tennessee, his flag was returned to Constance.

Hetty Cary spent the war years doing volunteer work in Richmond, Virginia, for the Confederate war effort. On January 19, 1865, Hetty married General John Pegram. Three weeks later, her new husband was killed in the Battle of Hatcher's Run.

soldiers would aim for the flag.

One Confederate flag bearer, Lieutenant P. E. Drew, was described by his fellow soldiers as "rushing into the jaws of death." Drew had picked up the banner from his company's fallen flag bearer and was racing into the Union line when he was shot through the heart. At Gettysburg, 14 flag bearers from one North Carolina regiment lost their lives in the course of the battle.

Today, the term "Color Guard" usually refers to the high school or college students who march at the front of their school's band in a parade, accompanying the colors. During the Civil War, the Color Guard was made up of a group of soldiers—usually a sergeant and five or more corporals—whose job during the battle was to protect the flag bearer and the flag. Members of the Color Guard had dangerous jobs. Many of them were killed protecting their flags.

Troops watching the advance of an army toward them always looked for the flag. If the flag appeared to be bouncing up and down, they knew the enemy was advancing toward them on the run. They called this type of advance "on the double quick."

There was no standard Confederate battle flag issued to every regiment throughout the war. Generals often tinkered with the size and shape of the flag. Many regimental leaders preferred a square flag to a rectangular

Each fighting unit of the Confederate Army had its own battle flag. This flag of the 11th Tennessee Regiment lists battles in which the regiment saw action.

banner. Some officers had the names of battles sewn into the flags to commemorate important victories by their units. Some generals preferred a white border to the flag while others favored an orange border. Sometimes, the stars were cut out of gold cloth.

General Stanhope Watie, the last Confederate general to surrender, had a flag made up that resembled the Stars and Bars, but the banner contained 16 stars in the blue field. Watie said the 16 stars stood for the 11 states that seceded from the Union and the five Indian nations that supported the South's war against the North. Across the central bar of the flag were the words "Cherokee Braves." Watie was three-quarters Cherokee and many members of his regiment were Indians.

Many states adopted what was known as the "Bonnie Blue Flag" during the war. This flag included just one

Belle Boyd had been a popular member of Washington society before the Civil War. During the war, she became a spy for the Confederacy, and displayed the flag outside her home in Virginia. On July 4, 1861, a group of Union soldiers spotted the flag and attempted to tear it down. They didn't get too far. Boyd shot the leader of the group, causing the other Union soldiers to flee. The Confederate flag remained in front of her home.

large white star against a field of blue. Single-starred flags were displayed to show the state had cut its ties with the union. The name "Bonnie Blue" came from a popular song named "Bonnie Blue" that was written

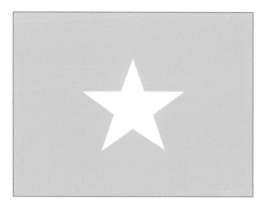

The Bonnie Blue flag.

and sung by a comedian named Harry McCarthy.

Women across the South were drafted to stitch the flags. One factory in Richmond employed some 2,000 Confederate women to sew uniforms for the soldiers as well as battle flags.

Civilians in the South were often willing to put their lives on the line for the flag as well. After New Orleans was captured by Union troops, General Benjamin F. Butler ordered the people of the city not to display symbols of the Confederacy. One woman responded by sewing a dress from the battle flag; she then strolled through the streets of the city in defiance of Butler's order. Butler had her arrested and thrown in prison.

A Confederate spy named Rose Greenhow smuggled a flag into her prison cell in Washington. Greenhow was said to have waved the flag from her cell window every day she was held in custody.

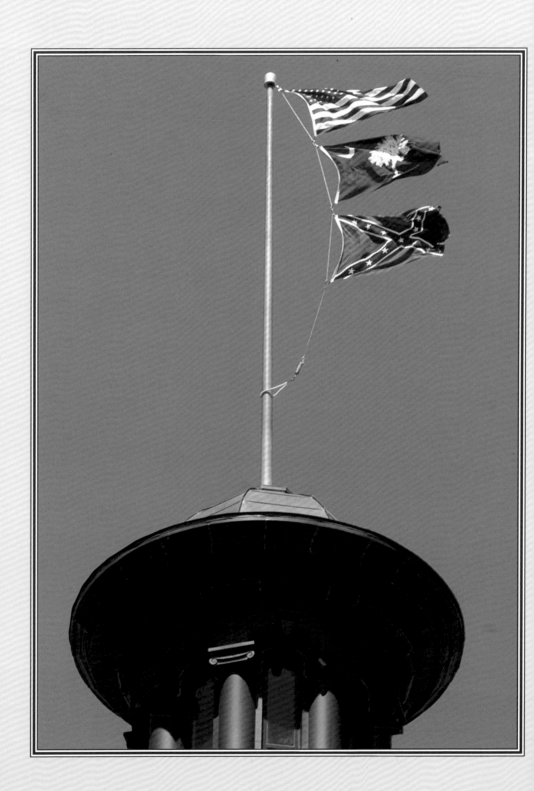

In this photo taken in April 2000, the Confederate flag flies over the South Carolina statehouse beneath the American flag and the state flag of South Carolina. The South Carolina State Senate voted to remove the Confederate battle flag from atop the Capitol dome on April 14, 2000—exactly 139 years after the Stars and Bars had been hoisted over Fort Sumter by victorious rebel soldiers.

HATRED OR HERITAGE?

Since the end of the Civil War, African Americans as well as others have regarded the Confederate flag as a symbol of hatred and racism. Over the years it has not been uncommon to see news reports on television that showed Confederate battle flags waved by members of the Ku Klux Klan, a racist organization.

But many white citizens of the South do not regard the Confederate flag as a symbol of racism. They feel it is an important symbol of their history and heritage, and that the flag represents the bravery and sacrifices of ancestors who they feel fought for a noble cause.

"It's a symbol of defiance, courage, and bravery," said

> Confederate battle flags captured by Union soldiers were held by the United States War Department until the early 1900s, when they were returned to the secessionist states.

Pat Buchanan, a political commentator who ran for president during the 2000 election. "Everyone should stand up for their heritage."

Others see the flag quite differently. Carol Mosley-Braun, a U.S. senator from Illinois, convinced the U.S. Congress to reject the insignia of the organization United Daughters of the Confederacy, which included the image of the Confederate flag.

"This is about race," said Mosley-Braun, an African American. "It is about racial symbols and the single most painful episode in American history."

In no place has the debate over the use of the Confederate flag been louder than in the states of Georgia, South Carolina, and Mississippi.

For years, the state flags of Georgia and Mississippi included images of the Confederate battle flag. In South Carolina, the battle flag flew atop the state Capitol dome right next to the state's official flag.

The story of Georgia's state flag dated back to July 1, 1956, when John Sammons Bell, a local political leader, convinced the state *legislature* to adopt a design for the flag that included an image of the state's official seal in a blue field on the inner third of the flag, while the rest of the flag contained an image of the Southern Cross battle flag. The Georgia flag also included the words "Wisdom, Justice, and Moderation."

But by the 1990s, black citizens of Georgia wanted to know why a symbol they considered racist should be allowed to fly over the state government's buildings. After several years of debate, black leaders in Georgia convinced the state legislature to adopt a new flag. Many descendants of Civil War veterans called on the legislature to resist the change, but, finally, on January 31, 2001, a new flag was hoisted over the Capitol. This design still featured an image of the Southern Cross, but on the new flag the cross is small and far less prominent than it had been before. "It's a beautiful blue sky and a beautiful flag going up," said Tyrone Brooks, a state legislator who had fought for more than a decade to alter the design of the Georgia state flag.

The new flag of Georgia flies beneath the U.S. flag outside the state house building. The redesigned flag features smaller versions of earlier Georgia flags, including one that contains the Confederate battle flag. The new flag was hoisted over the capital in January 2001.

South Carolina's state flag includes no image of the Southern Cross—the flag contains the images of a palmetto tree and crescent moon against a blue field. But in 1962, South Carolina legislators ordered the Confederate battle flag flown atop the Capitol dome alongside the state flag to mark the 100th anniversary of the Civil War. At the end of the *centennial*, the Southern Cross stayed atop the dome.

Members of the National Association for the Advancement of Colored People (NAACP) pressured South Carolina's legislators to take down the battle flag.

A man holds up a sign protesting the Confederate flag flying over the South Carolina statehouse in July 2000. A few moments after this photo was taken, the flag was officially removed from the government building. It now flies over a nearby cemetery.

In early 2000, the NAACP urged its members not to travel in South Carolina or take vacations there. South Carolina gets a lot of money from tourists who visit the state's coastal towns and beaches. Tourism officials estimated that in the first month the NAACP *boycott* had cost businesses in South Carolina about $7 million.

South Carolina's political leaders finally relented, and on July 1, 2000, the Confederate flag came down from the Capitol dome. But the flag's supporters did win a compromise. They won approval to raise the battle flag over a nearby cemetery for Confederate soldiers.

Mississippians also faced questions about hatred and heritage when they went to the polls on April 17, 2001, to vote on a *referendum* that would decide whether a new flag would fly over their State House in Jackson. For 107 years, the state flag of Mississippi included the Southern Cross in its upper left corner.

For Mississippi, the first indication that black citizens opposed the battle flag came in 1983, when African American students at the University of Mississippi asked school officials to stop using the Southern Cross as the school's official symbol. University officials soon lowered the rebel flags that flew over the campus.

After that, black leaders in Mississippi called for

> In many communities in the South, March 4 is celebrated as "Confederate Flag Day." The battle flag is also flown in many southern cities on January 19— Robert E. Lee's birthday.

removal of the flag atop the Capitol as well. Finally, in January 2001 Governor Ronnie Musgrove signed a bill authorizing the referendum. Voters had the opportunity to choose the old 1894 flag or select a new design that substituted a blue field of stars for the Southern Cross.

For the next four months, the issue divided the citizens of Mississippi. One person who spoke on the issue was former Mississippi Governor William Winter, whose grandfather had served in the Confederate Army. Winter said, "I share that deep sense of history; I understand how many feel. But I also feel a flag—a flag that represents a people, a whole state, ought to be a symbol of unity, not division."

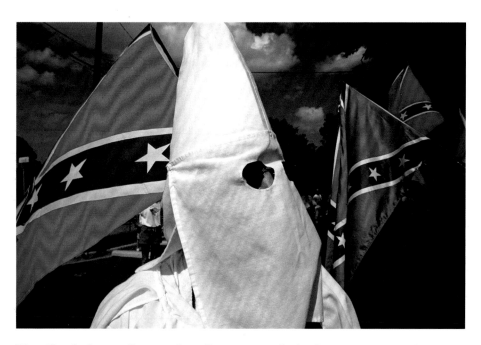

The Confederate flag is often flown proudly by hate groups such as the Ku Klux Klan. These groups use the flag to intimidate African Americans and other minorities.

On April 17, 2001, Mississippi voters decided to keep the Confederate battle flag as part of their state flag.

Finally, the citizens of Mississippi voted. By a clear majority, the voters decided to keep the symbol of the Southern Cross on their flag.

"I'm for the Confederate flag now and forever," said Shelby Foote, an author from Mississippi who has written several books on the Civil War. "Many among the finest people this country has ever produced died in that war."

1860 Abraham Lincoln elected president in November; in December seven states—South Carolina, Mississippi, Florida, Alabama, Georgia, Louisiana, and Texas—declare they are withdrawing from the U.S. to form a new country—the Confederate States of America.

1861 Stars and Bars is raised above the state Capitol in Montgomery, Alabama, on March 4; Confederate troops fire on Union-held Fort Sumter in South Carolina on April 12, touching off the Civil War; at Manassas, Virginia, on July 21, General Beauregard decides a new battle flag is needed when, in the heat of battle, he is unable to distinguish the Stars and Bars from the Stars and Stripes.

1863 Confederate Congress replaces the Stars and Bars with the Stainless Banner as the official flag of the Confederacy on May 1; the Civil War begins to turn in favor of the Union side with the Confederate defeat at Gettysburg July 1-3, and the fall of Vicksburg, an important city on the Mississippi River, on July 4.

1865 A red bar is added to the Stainless Banner on March 8; on April 9, General Robert E. Lee surrenders to General Ulysses S. Grant in Appomattox, Virginia, ending the Civil War; the Confederate ship *Shenandoah* arrives in Liverpool, England, and lowers the Confederate battle flag from its mast on November 6.

1894 Legislators in Mississippi adopt a state flag featuring the Southern Cross in the upper left corner on February 7.

1956 Georgia adopts a state flag that includes the Southern Cross on July 1.

1962 The South Carolina Legislature orders the Southern Cross flown atop the Capitol next to the state flag.

1983 Black students at the University of Mississippi convince school officials to drop the Southern Cross as the symbol of the university.

2000 NAACP leads a tourism boycott of South Carolina on January 1; the Southern Cross is removed from the Capitol dome in South Carolina on July 1 and displayed in a military cemetery on the Capitol grounds.

2001 Georgia adopts a new state flag featuring a small and less prominent Southern Cross on January 31; voters in Mississippi turn down a referendum to remove the Southern Cross from the state flag on April 17.

boycott—to refuse to deal with a person or group, in order to show disapproval or force acceptance of certain conditions.

bunting—a lightweight fabric used for flags and decorations.

capital—the city that serves as official center of government for a state or nation.

Capitol—a building located in the capital where the government passes laws and conducts other business.

casualties—soldiers wounded, captured, or killed in battle.

centennial—a 100th anniversary.

Confederacy—short for Confederate States of America, an organization of the 11 Southern states that seceded from the United States in 1860 and 1861.

Congress—the lawmaking branch of the federal government.

constellation—a group of stars that forms a familiar pattern.

delegate—a person designated to represent others, often at a political meeting or convention.

halyard—rope used to hoist a flag up a pole.

legislature—the lawmaking branch of a state government.

masthead—the print across the top of a newspaper's front page that displays the newspaper's name.

president—the chief executive of a country whose authority to govern is provided by vote of the citizens.

referendum—a vote by the people on a law proposed by a government body.

regiment—a military unit of infantry or cavalry soldiers.

seamstress—a woman whose occupation is sewing.

secede—to withdraw from an organization.

strategies—a series of plans intended to complete a wide-scale military maneuver.

tactics—maneuvers designed to position a military force for a specific attack.

vessel—a large ship.

FURTHER READING

Davis, William C. *A Government of Our Own: The Making of the Confederacy*. New York: The Free Press, 1994.

Elsner, Alan. "Confederate Flag Is Likely to Wave on over Mississippi." *The Philadelphia Inquirer*, April 14, 2001.

Foote, Shelby. *The Civil War, a Narrative*. New York: Random House, 1974.

Garrison, Webb. *Civil War Curiosities*. Nashville, Tenn.: Rutledge Hill Press, 1994.

Hoffman, Kathryn. "A New Flag for Georgia." *Time for Kids*, February 9, 2001.

Horwitz, Tony. "A Death for Dixie." *The New Yorker*, March 18, 1996.

LaHay, Patricia M. "New Georgia Flag Hoisted Above Statehouse." *The Washington Post*, January 31, 2001.

Owen, Richard, and James Owen. *Generals at Rest*. Shippensburg, Pa.: White Mane Publishing Company, 1997.

Parrish, Thomas. *The American Flag*. New York: Simon and Schuster, 1973.

INTERNET RESOURCES

Confederate Battle Flag
http://www.fotw.stm.it/flags/us-csa.html
http://www.researchonline.net/gacw/confla.12.htm

Confederate Flag's Last Day over South Carolina Capitol
http://www.CNN.com
http://www.ABCnews.com

History of the Stars and Bars
http://www.freedixie.net/heritage/2natflag.html
http://www.americancivilwar.com/south/conflag/ southflg.html

PICTURE CREDITS

BARRY MORENO has been librarian and historian at the Ellis Island Immigration Museum and the Statue of Liberty National Monument since 1988. He is the author of *The Statue of Liberty Encyclopedia*, which was published by Simon and Schuster in October 2000. He is a native of Los Angeles, California. After graduation from California State University at Los Angeles, where he earned a degree in history, he joined the National Park Service as a seasonal park ranger at the Statue of Liberty; he eventually became the monument's librarian. In his spare time, Barry enjoys reading, writing, and studying foreign languages and grammar. His biography has been included in *Who's Who Among Hispanic Americans*, *The Directory of National Park Service Historians*, *Who's Who in America*, and *The Directory of American Scholars*.

HAL MARCOVITZ is a journalist for *The Morning Call*, a newspaper based in Allentown, Pennsylvania. He has written more than 20 books for young readers. He lives in Chalfont, Pennsylvania, with his wife, Gail, and their daughters, Ashley and Michelle.